Chinese Word Book

Illustrated by
Jiang An

The Bess Press
P.O. Box 22388
Honolulu, HI 96822

Executive Editor: Ann Rayson
Design & Illustration: Jiang An

Library of Congress

CATALOG CARD NO.: 89-82132

An, Jiang
Chinese Word Book
Honolulu, Hawaii: Bess Press
112 pages   illustration, glossary-Chinese-English, English-Chinese

Table of Contents

Pronunciation Guide

The Chinese Language

Written Chinese does not use letters of the alphabet. Instead, Chinese is written in characters that began as pictographs, that were developed thousands of years ago. During the intervening years these pictures were simplified and standardized so that most of them no longer look anything like objects. For example, the word for "man" has changed in this way 冬 冬 冬 人 人 . And the word for "mountain" has gone through this change 山 山 山 .

Chinese words are represented by characters, singly or in combination. Although two different words may sound entirely alike, they are generally written with different characters. To learn to read and write in Chinese one must memorize thousands of different symbols. But learning to speak Chinese is much easier because the sounds can be written with the letters of the Romanized alphabet by using the *pinyin* system of transliteration. There are, of course, other systems of transliteration, but pinyin is now the most widely used alphabet system. It is often used in Chinese schools for beginners who have not yet mastered written characters. We have used this system throughout the book, along with the written characters for those who would like to begin learning to read the symbols.

How To Say Chinese Words

Every Chinese word has a special tone, or pitch. The tones are quite important. Words that have the same sound (that is, are spelled the same way in the phonetic alphabet) will have different tones and therefore different meanings. This gives the language a musical quality. For example, the word <u>ma</u> when pronounced with the 1st (or high) tone means mother. <u>Ma</u> pronounced with a rising tone means hemp. <u>Ma</u> pronounced with a falling and then rising tone means horse, and <u>ma</u> pronounced with just a falling tone means to scold someone.

There are four of these tones in Mandarin Chinese.

1st, high and level (marked ‾ above the main vowel)
2nd, rising, (marked /)
3rd, falling and then rising (marked ∪)
4th, falling (marked \)

Other sounds that may seem strange are:
C which sounds like the final ts in dots or students
R which sounds like the ur in leisure and pleasure
Q which sounds like ch in cheer or chin
X which sounds like sh in shell or shoe
Z which sounds like ds in reads or seeds
CH which sounds like the final ch in church and peach
ENG which sounds like sung
IAN which sounds like yen
UI which sounds like way
ZH which sounds like dg in judge or dodge

Foreword

Mandarin is the most widely used form of the Chinese language. It is spoken by one quarter of the world's population. Chinese is also a very ancient language, long predating English. The appearance of Chinese characters was standardized during the Wei and Jin Dynasties (221 A.D.–580 A.D.), and only small changes have been made since.

In this book many basic Chinese words are presented for both children and adults interested in learning the Chinese language. Every word includes both romanized (*pinyin*) and character formats.

An illustration accompanies each word to make it easier to learn. The attractive and sometimes humorous illustrations are by Jiang An, a favorite illustrator of children's books in China.

Chinese writing has no alphabet and every word is represented by a different character, so that thousands of separate representations must be memorized in order to be able to read the language. (An unabridged Chinese dictionary may contain as many as 60,000 different Chinese characters.) But it is not difficult to learn to speak Chinese with the help of romanization. There are several romanization systems, but pinyin is used exclusively today in China and so we have chosen to use it also. It is the alphabetized form of Chinese that any reader will encounter most commonly. In this book we have also included (for every word) the simplified form of the Chinese characters that has been in use throughout China during the past forty years.

Spoken Chinese uses voice tones to show the difference between words that otherwise would sound alike. In Mandarin Chinese there are only four of these tones: high, rising, dipping, and falling. When the pinyin system is used, these tones are marked with four different types of lines above the vowels (see the Pronunciation Guide at the back of the book). At first this may seem difficult, but with a little practice it becomes simple.

The words in this book represent those that language teachers have identified as ones that frequently appear in daily conversation, newspapers, and simple written texts. They are only a beginning for the study of Chinese, but mastery of them will greatly enhance the process of learning and connect you with over a billion people in the world who speak this language.

Fu Sita
Editor of Chinese–English language texts

Social Life and Relations

nánrén	yéye	dàye
nǚrén	nǎinai	yímā
rénmén	fùqīn	gōngrén
nǚháizi	mǔqīn	nóngmín
nánháizi	érzi	lǎoshī
yīngér	nǚér	

男人 nánrén

man

女人 nǚrén

woman

人们 rénmén

人們 people

男孩子
nánháizi
boy

女孩子 nǚháizi
girl

婴儿
嬰兒
yīngér
baby

5

爷爷
爺爺
yéye
grandfather

奶奶
nǎinai
grandmother

大爷 大爺
dàye
uncle

姨妈 姨媽
yímā
aunt

7

母亲
母親
muqīn

mother

儿子
兒子
érzi

son

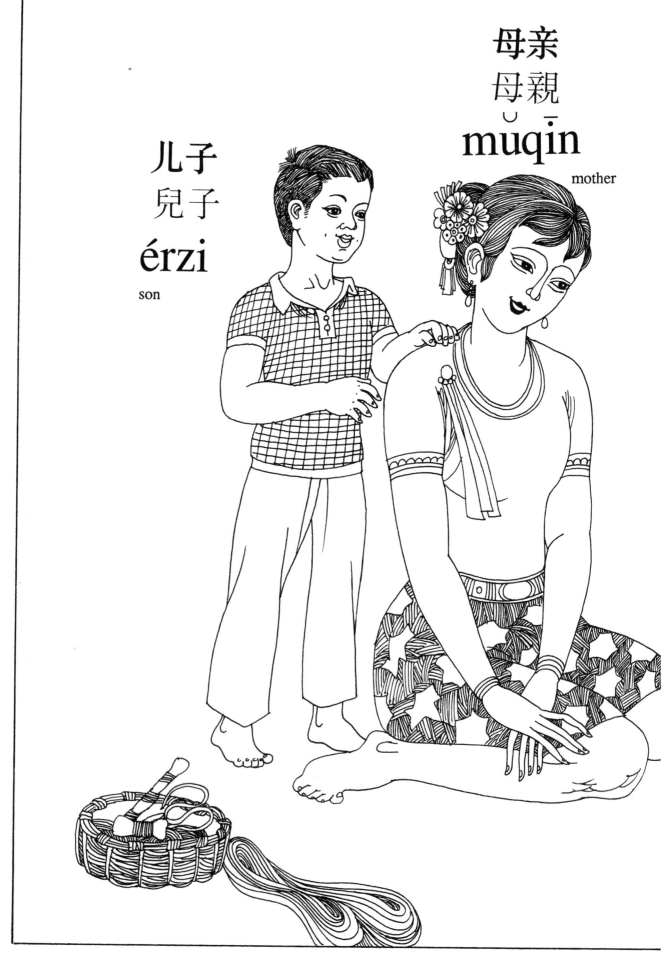

父亲
父親
fùqīn

father

女儿
女兒
nǚér

daughter

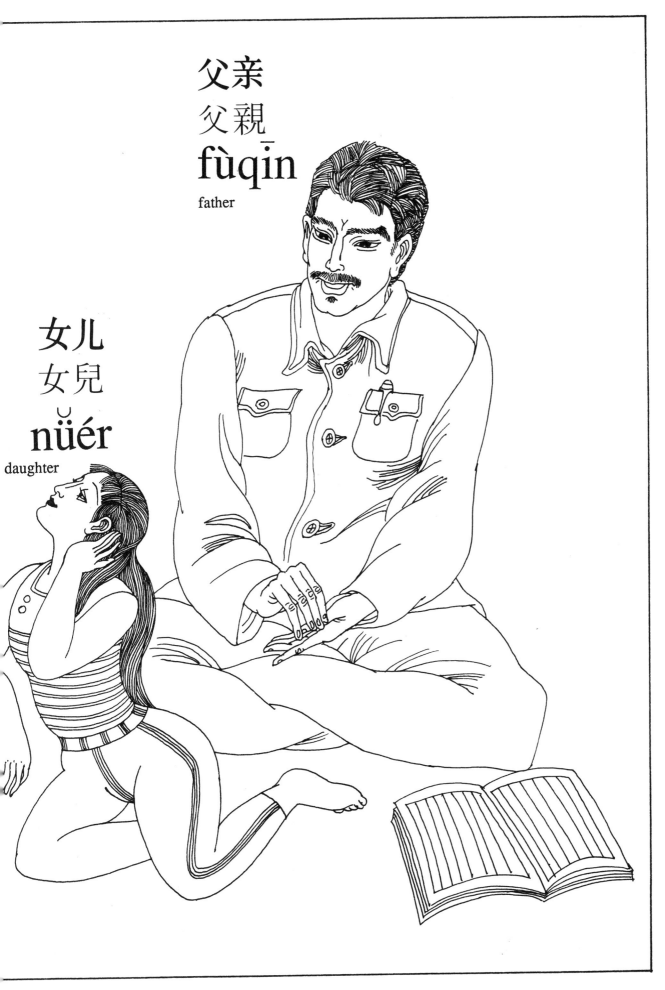

9

工人 gōngrén

worker

农民 nóngmín
農民 farmer

11

老师
老師 lǎoshī
teacher

Chinese Lifestyle

miào	nóngchǎng	shōuyīnjī
tǎ	Chángchéng	gōnggòng qìchē
chǎngfáng	diànhuà	xiǎoqìchē
chéngshì	diànshìjī	

塔 tǎ

pagoda

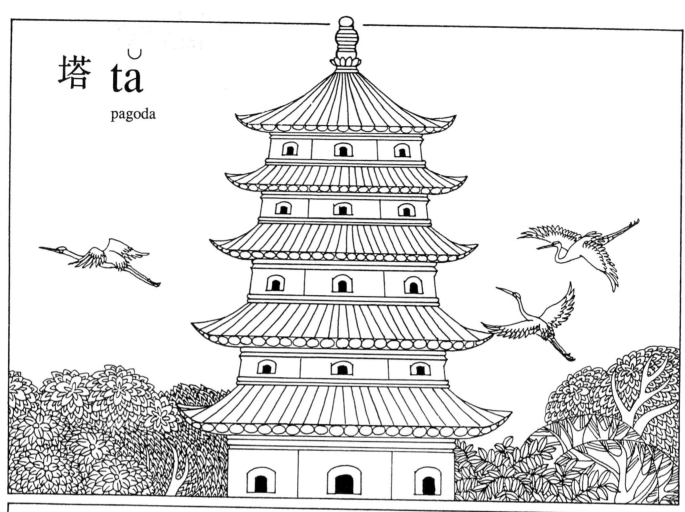

庙
廟

miào

temple

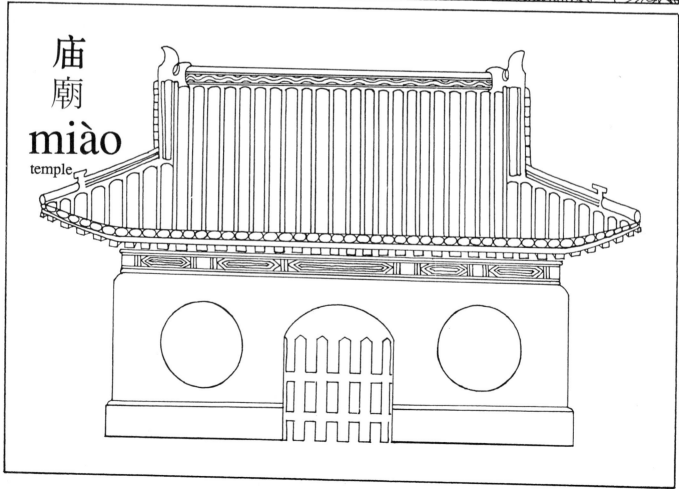

14

城市 city
chéngshì

厂房 廠房
chǎngfáng
factory

15

农场 nóngchǎng
農場 farm

长城 Chángchéng
The Great Wall

电话 diànhuà telephone
電話

shōuyīnjī 收音机
radio 收音機

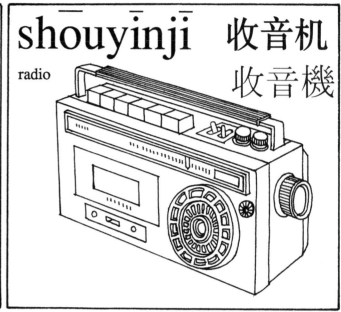

电视机 diànshìjī
電視機 television

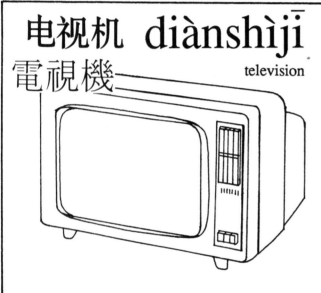

小汽车 xiǎoqìchē
小汽車 car

公共汽车 gōnggòng qìchē
公共汽車 bus

Human Body

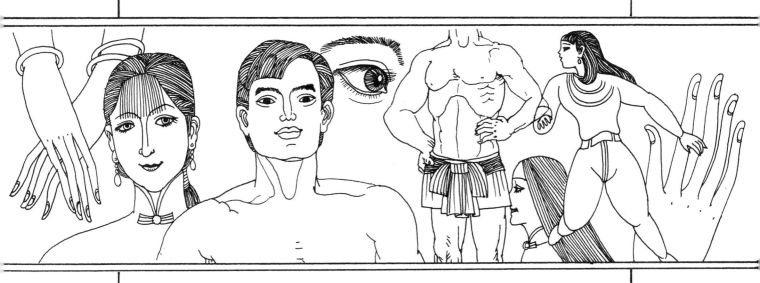

tóu	jiān	jiǎozhǐ
shēntǐ	xiōngkǒu	jīgǔ
tóufa	gēbo	xīnzàng
yǎnjīng	shǒu	bèi
bízi	shǒuzhǐ	gān
zuǐ	tuǐ	chángzi
ěrduō	xī	wèi
xiàba	jiǎo	

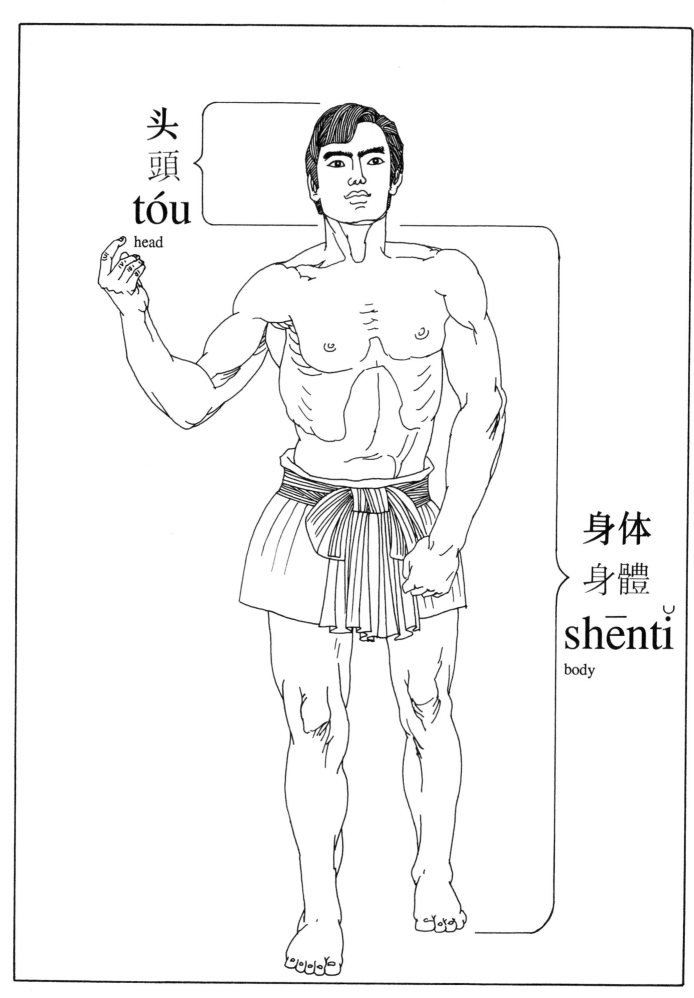

头
頭
tóu
head

身体
身體
shēntǐ
body

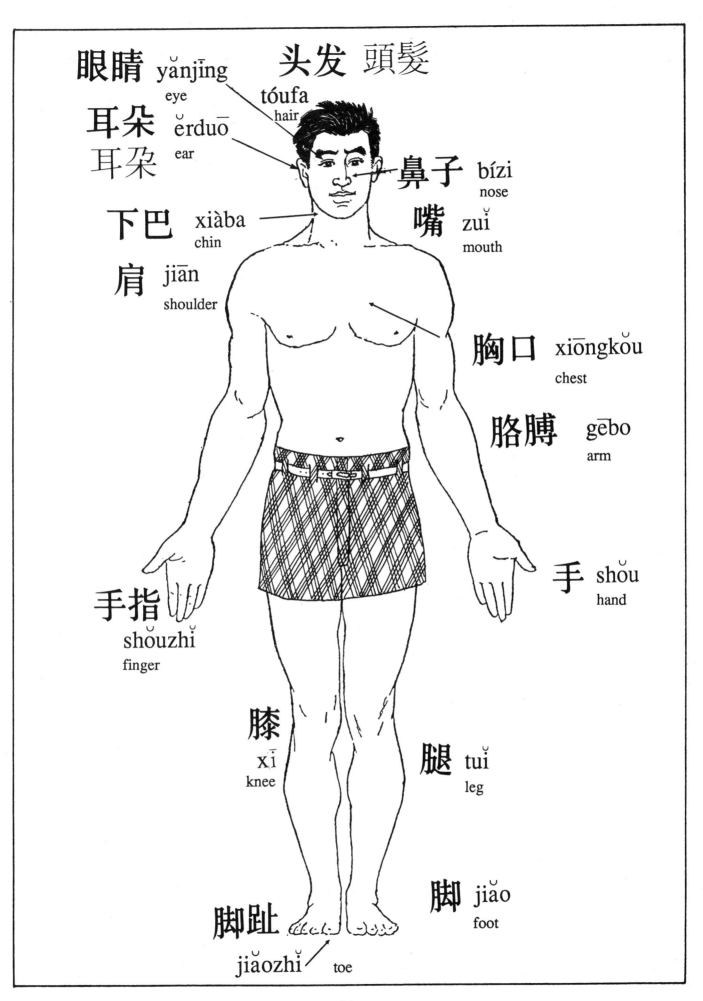

眼睛 yǎnjīng
eye

耳朵 ěrduō
耳朵 ear

下巴 xiàba
chin

肩 jiān
shoulder

头发 頭髮
tóufa
hair

鼻子 bízi
nose

嘴 zuǐ
mouth

胸口 xiōngkǒu
chest

胳膊 gēbo
arm

手 shǒu
hand

手指
shǒuzhǐ
finger

膝
xī
knee

腿 tuǐ
leg

脚 jiǎo
foot

脚趾
jiǎozhǐ   toe

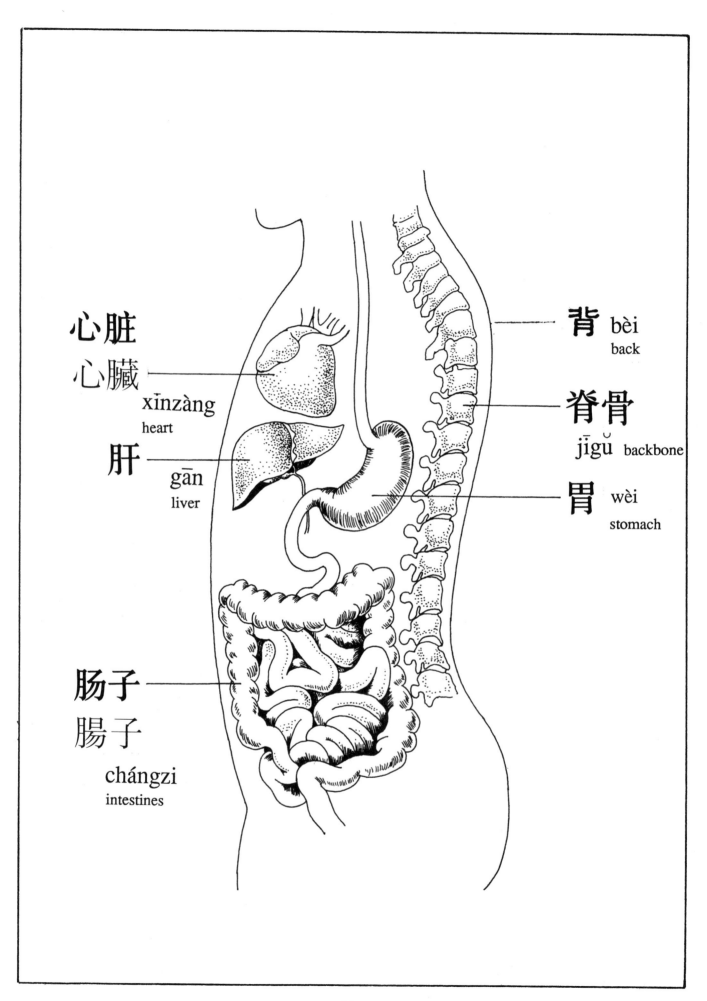

心脏
心臟
xīnzàng
heart

肝
gān
liver

肠子
腸子
chángzi
intestines

背 bèi
back

脊骨
jǐgǔ backbone

胃 wèi
stomach

Food

hē	kuàizi	júzǐ
pǐncháng	miànbāo	xiāngjiāo
zhū	tāng	chāzi
yú	chá	pánzi
jī	shuǐ	sháozi
yā	jīdàn	bōlí bēi
mǐfàn	píngguǒ	cānjīn

喝　hē
drink

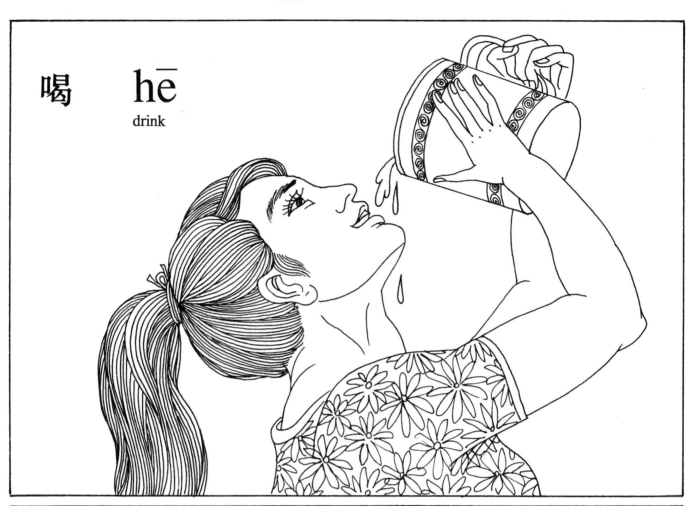

品尝 pǐncháng
品嘗 taste

鱼 yú
魚
fish

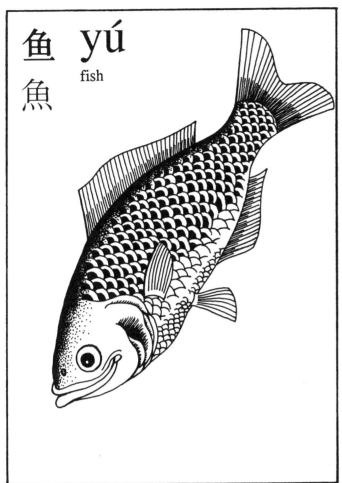

猪 zhū
pig

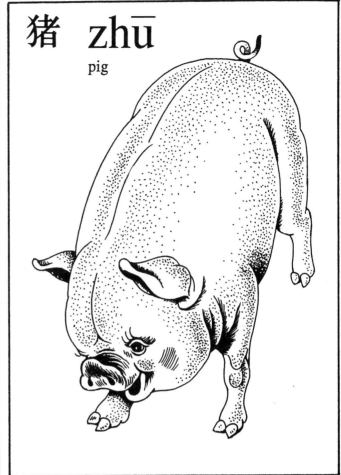

鸡 jī chicken
雞

鸭 yā duck
鴨

米饭 **mǐfàn**
米飯 rice

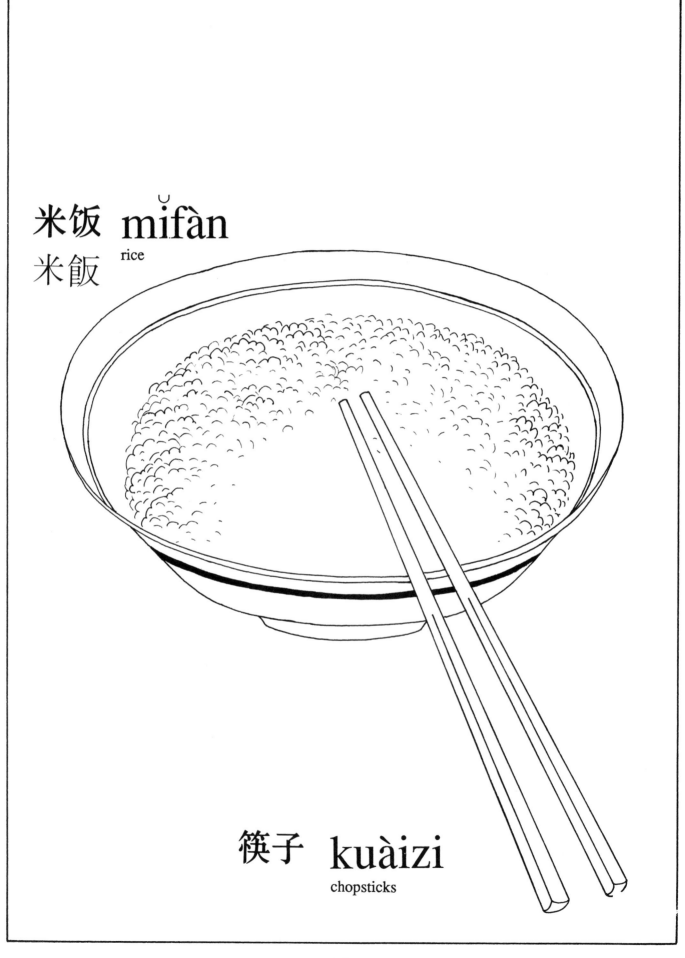

筷子 **kuàizi**
chopsticks

面包 miànbāo
麵包

bread

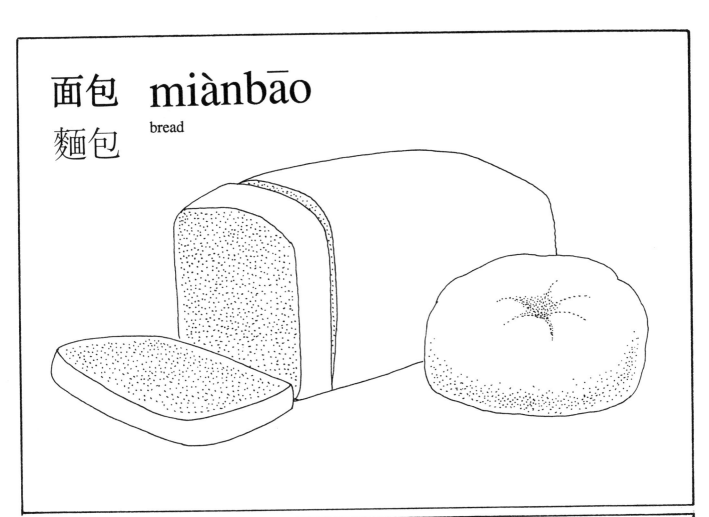

汤 tāng
湯

soup

茶 chá
tea

水 shuǐ
water

鸡蛋 jīdàn
雞蛋　　eggs

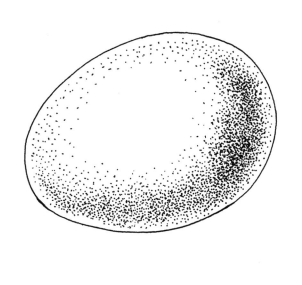

苹果 píngguǒ
蘋果　　apple

桔子 júzi
橘子　　orange

香蕉 xiāngjiāo
banana

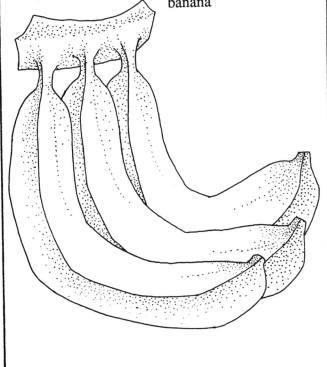

29

玻璃杯 bōlí bēi

glass

勺子 sháozi

spoon

餐巾 cānjīn

napkin

盘子 pánzi

盤子

plate

叉子 chāzi

fork

30

Clothing

màozi	kùzi	zhūbǎo
xié	yǎnjìng	shǒujuàn
chènyī	chángtǒng wà	qiánbāo

帽子 màozi
hat

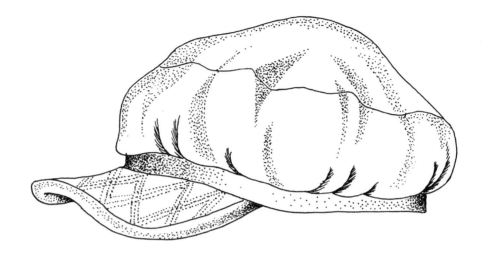

鞋 xié
shoes

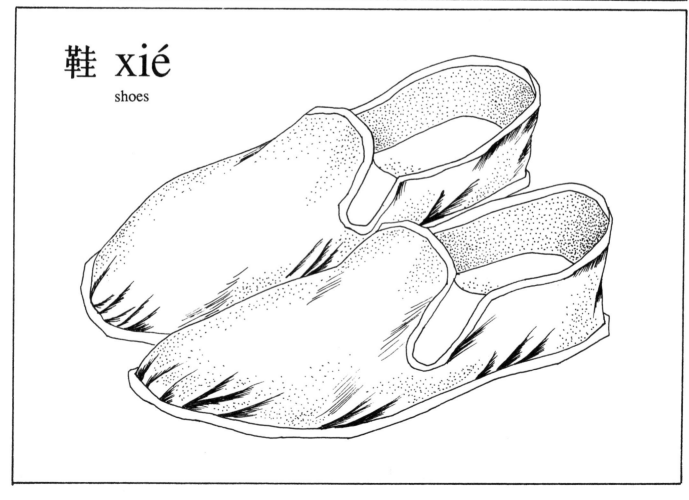

衬衣 chènyī
襯衣 shirt

裤子 kùzi
褲子 trousers

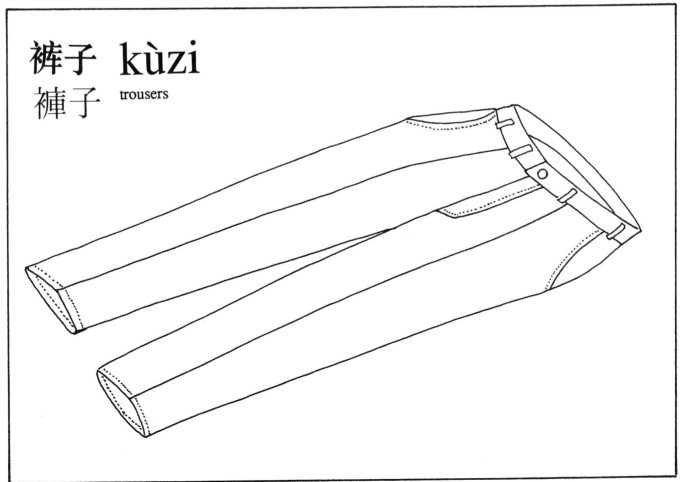

长筒袜

長筒襪

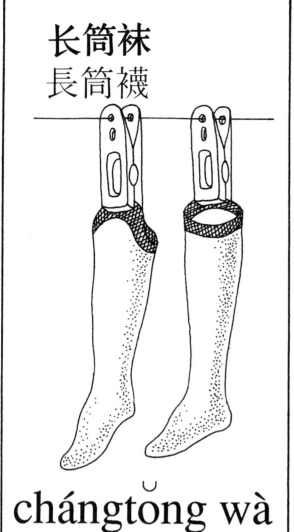

chángtǒng wà

stockings

眼镜 **yǎnjìng**

眼鏡　　glasses

钱包 **qiánbāo**

錢包　　purse

珠宝 **zhūbǎo**

珠寶　　jewelry

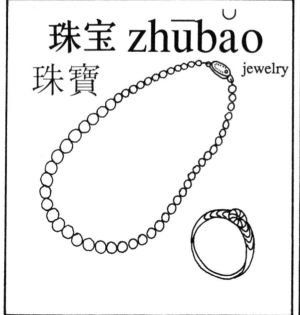

手绢 **shǒujuàn**

手絹　handkerchief

House

zhĕntóu   mén   fángzi

chuáng   chuānghù jiā

zhuōzi   tănzi

房子
fángzi

building

门 門
mén

gate

家 jiā

house

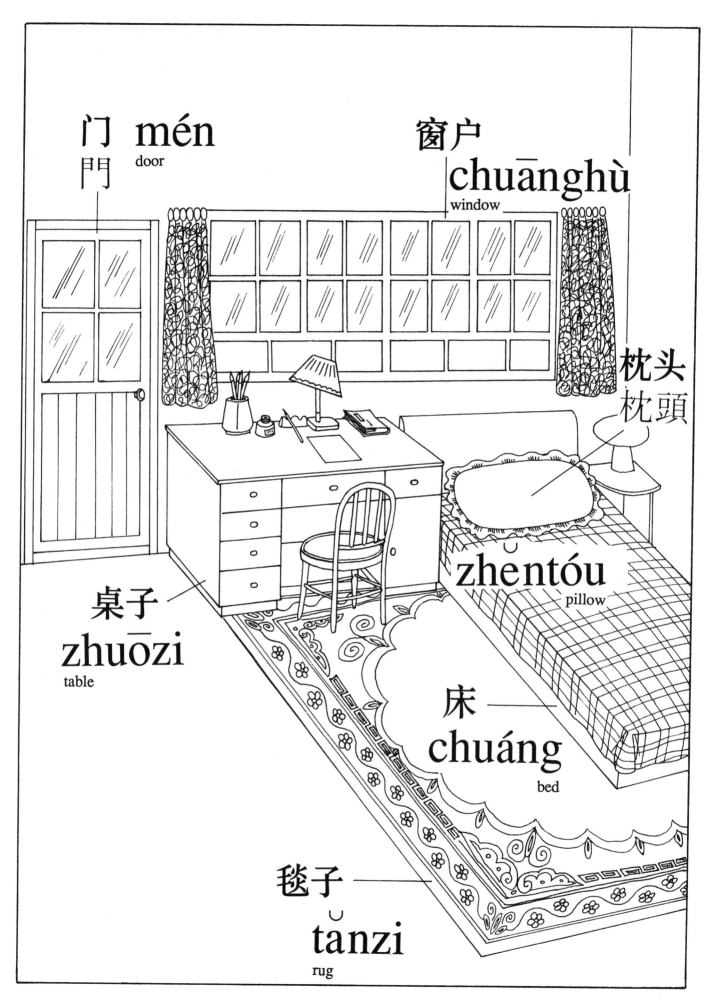

门 mén
門
door

窗户
chuānghù
window

枕头
枕頭
zhěntóu
pillow

桌子
zhuōzi
table

床
chuáng
bed

毯子
tǎnzi
rug

Actions

gěi	pǎo	dǒng
lái	tiào	gōngzuò
qù	zǒu	shuō
zhàn	yóuyǒng	shǔ
zuò	tǐng	
tǎngxià	kàn	

给 gěi

給 give

来 lái
come

去 qù
go

站 zhàn
stand

坐 zuò
sit

躺下 tǎngxià
lie down

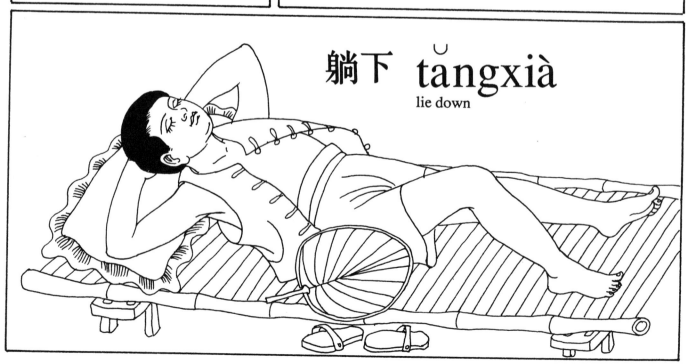

跑 pǎo

run

跳 tiào

jump

走 zǒu

walk

游泳 yóuyǒng

swim

听 tīng

聽 listen

听 tīng

聽 hear

看 **kàn**

see

懂 **dǒng**

understand

工作 gōngzuò

work

说 **shuō**
说
speak

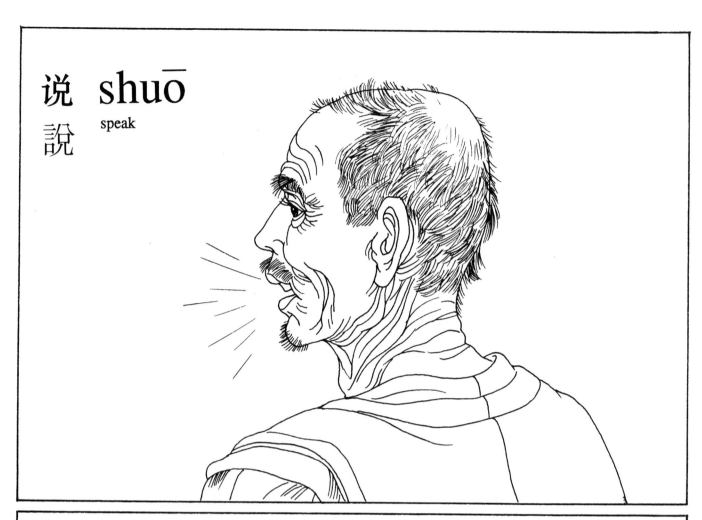

数 **shǔ**
數
count

Opposites

shòu	rè	dà
pàng	lěng	xiǎo
měi	gāo	jìn
chǒu	ǎi	yuǎn
gāoxìng	xīn	zhòng
bù gāoxìng	jiù	qīng

瘦 shòu
thin

胖 pàng
胖 fat

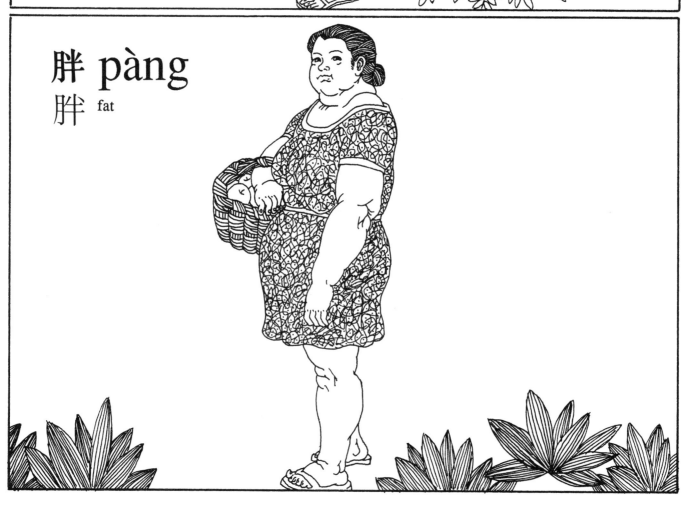

美 měi

beautiful

丑 chǒu
醜

ugly

高兴 gāoxìng
高興 happy

不高兴 bù gāoxìng
不高興 sad

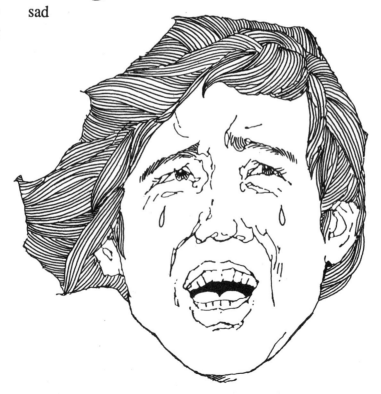

热 rè
熱
hot

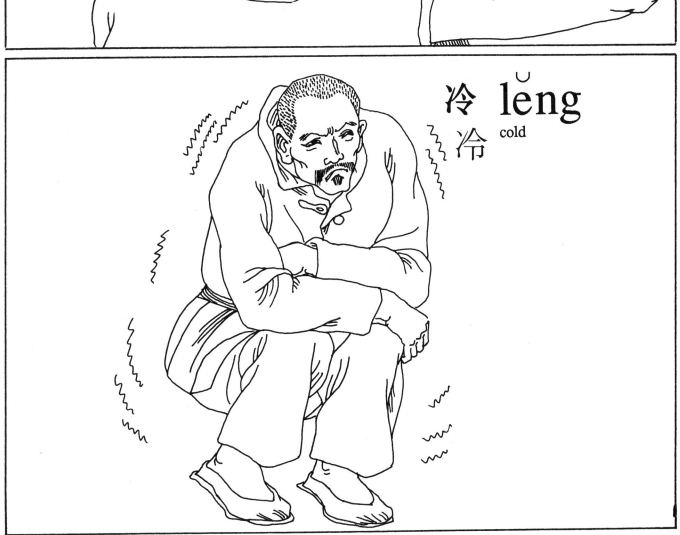

冷 lěng
冷
cold

高 gāo
tall

矮 ǎi
short

54

新 xīn
new

旧 jiù
舊 old

大 dà
big

小 xiǎo
small

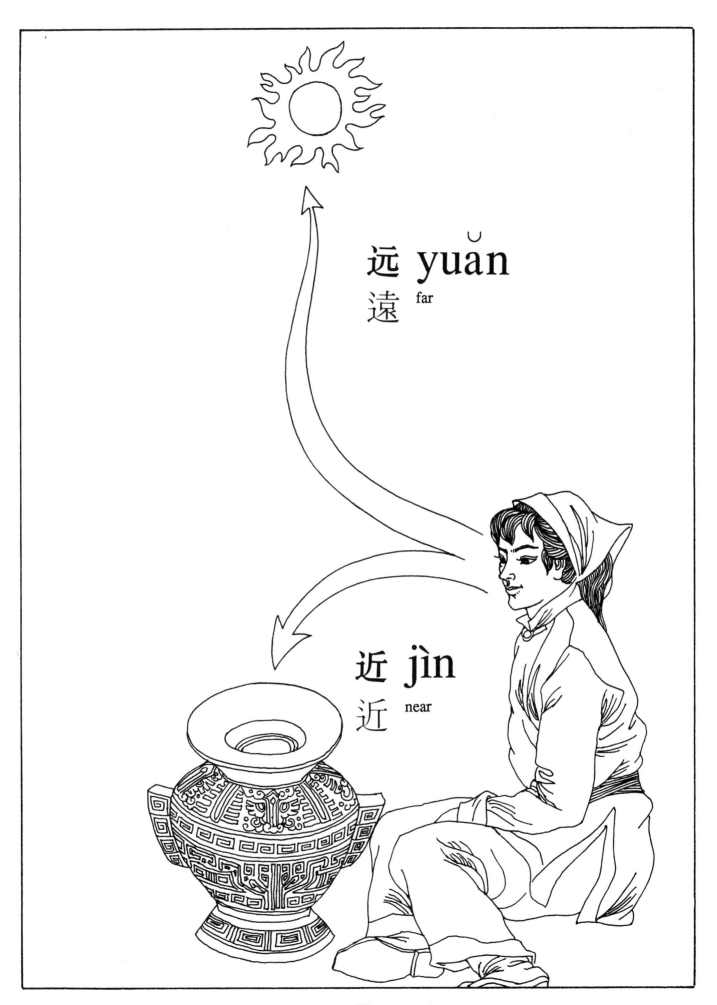

远 yuǎn
遠 far

近 jìn
近 near

57

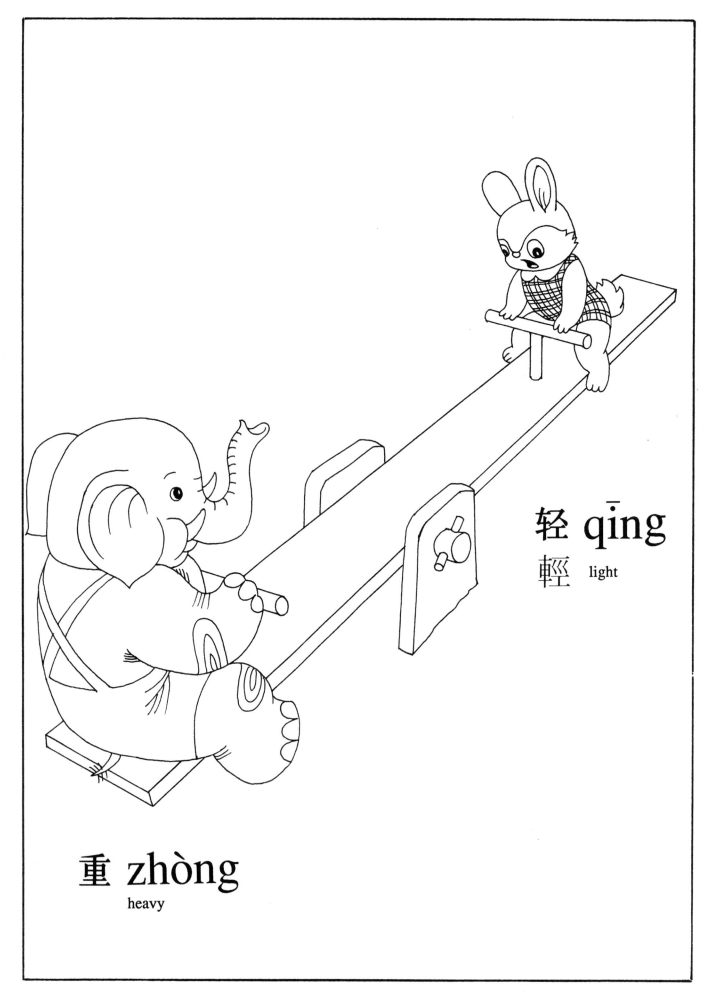

轻 qīng
輕 light

重 zhòng
heavy

Locations

qiánbiān
zhōngjiān
hòubiān

shàngbiān
xiàbiān
lǐbiān

wàibiān
xiān
hòu

前边 **qiánbiān**
前邊 in front

中间
中間
zhōngjiān
between

后边
後邊
hòubiān
behind

上边 shàngbiān
上邊 above

下边 xiàbiān
下邊 below

里边 lǐbiān
裏邊 in

外边 wàibiān
外邊 out

后 hòu
先 last

先 xiān
後 first

Numbers

yī	qī	líng
èr	bā	èrshí
sān	jiǔ	yìbǎi
sì	shí	yìqiān
wǔ	shíyí	yíwàn
liù	shíèr	

— **1** yī
one

= **2** èr
two

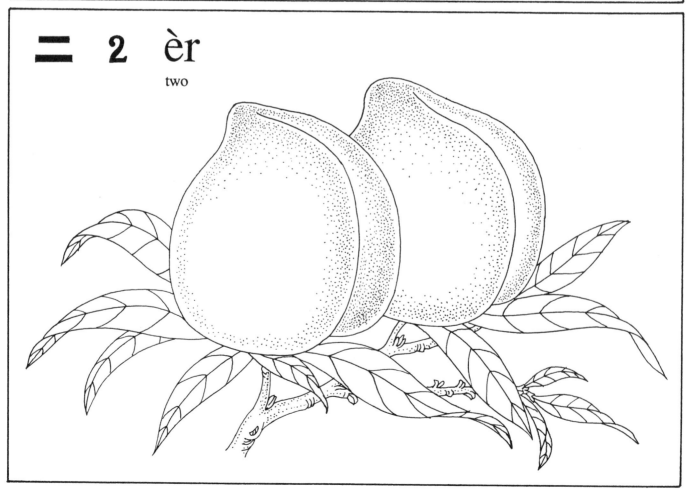

三 **3 sān**
three

四 **4 sì**
four

五 **5 wǔ**
five

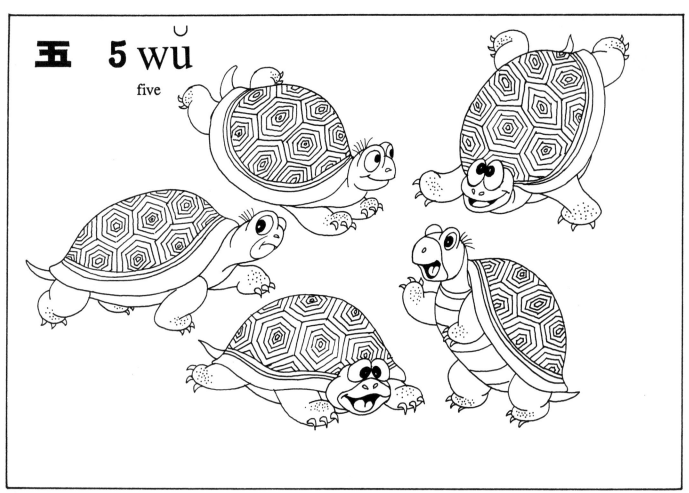

六 **6 liù**
six

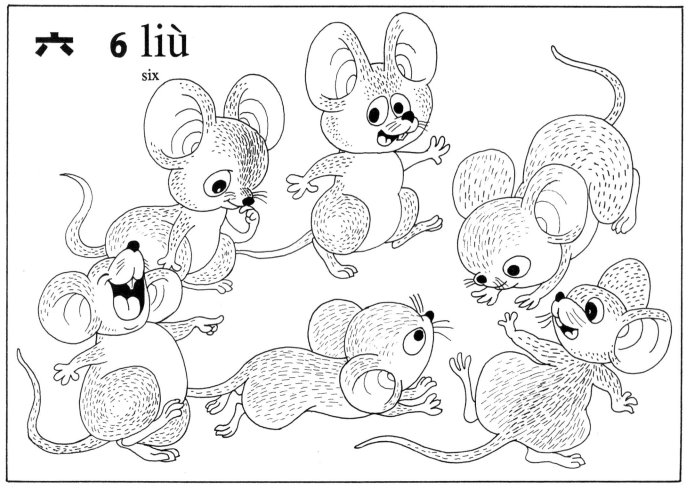

七 **7** qī seven

八 **8** bā eight

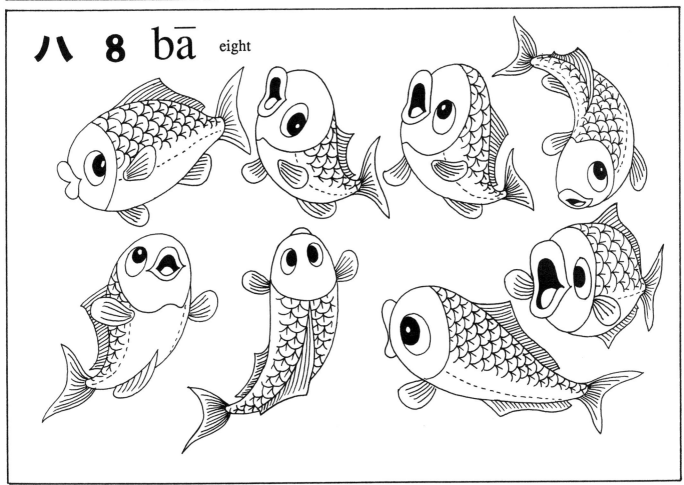

69

九 **9** jiǔ
nine

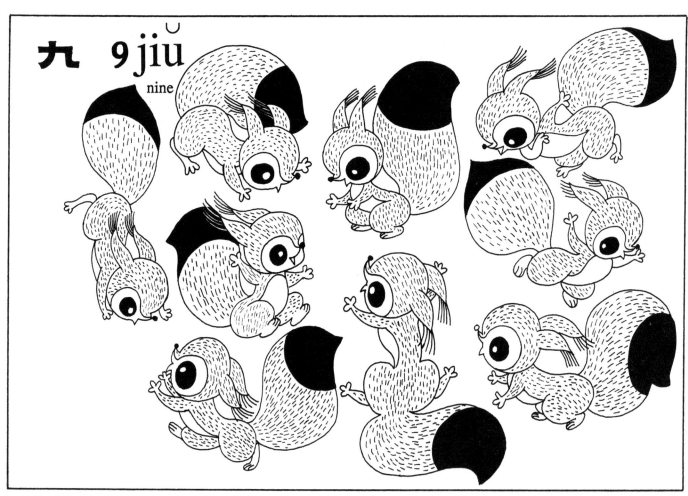

十 **10** shí
ten

+ − 11 shíyī eleven

+ = 12 shíèr twelve

71

零 零
líng
zero

0

二十
èrshí
twenty

20

一百
yìbǎi
one hundred

100

一千
yìqiān
one thousand

1000

一万
一萬
yíwàn
ten thousand

10000

In the Classroom

yǐzi	qiānbǐ	fěnbǐ
shūzhuō	gāngbǐ	shū
dìtú	hēibǎncā	jiùzhǐlǒu
túhuà	zhǐ	
hēibǎn	zhōng	

书桌 shūzhuō
書桌 desk

椅子 yǐzi
chair

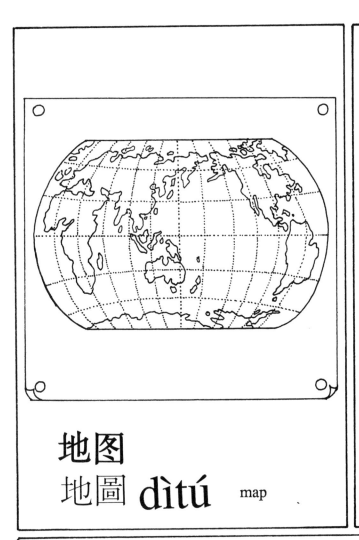

地图
地圖 dìtú   map

图画
圖畫 túhuà   picture

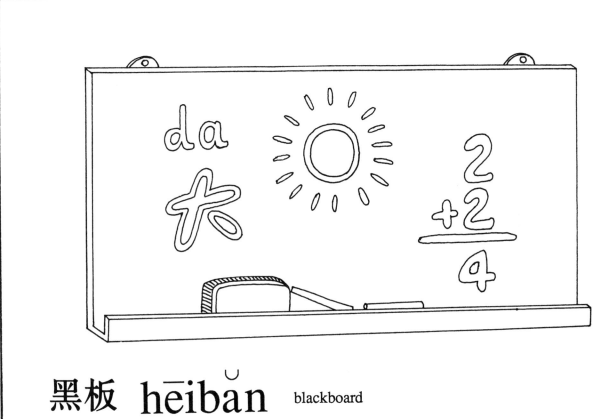

黑板 hēibǎn   blackboard

铅笔 qiānbǐ
鉛筆 pencil

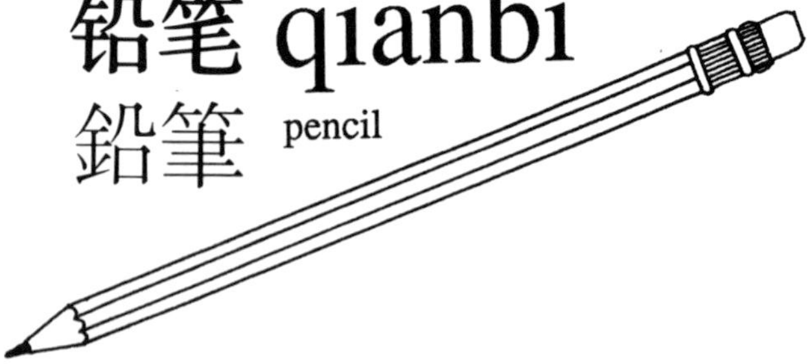

钢笔
鋼筆

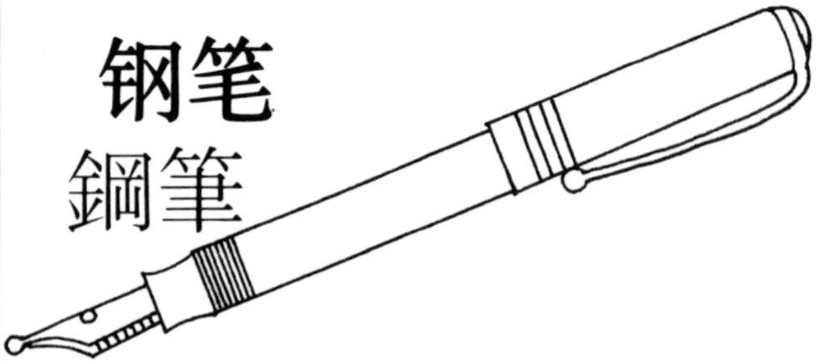

gāngbǐ pen

黑板擦

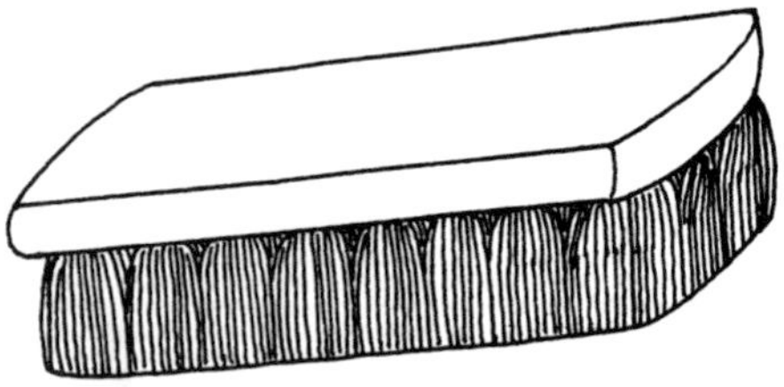

hēibǎncā eraser

纸
紙

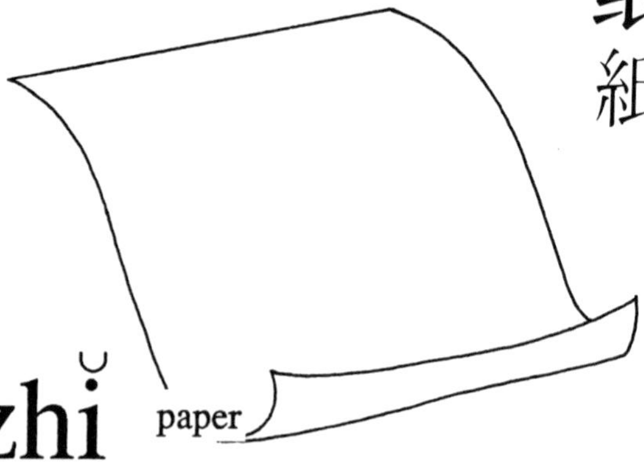

zhǐ paper

钟
鐘

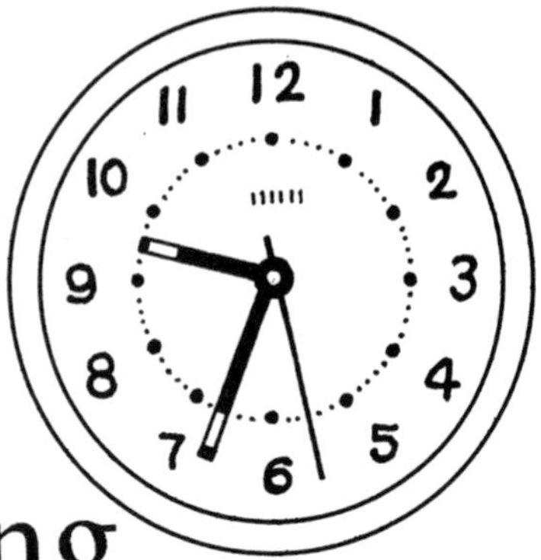

zhōng clock

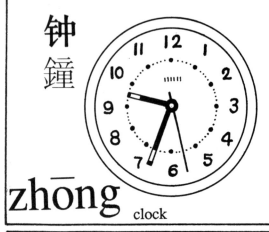

粉笔
粉筆

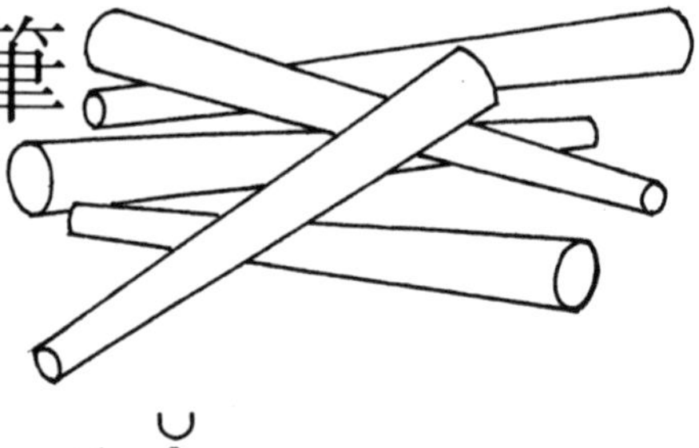

fěnbǐ chalk

shū
book

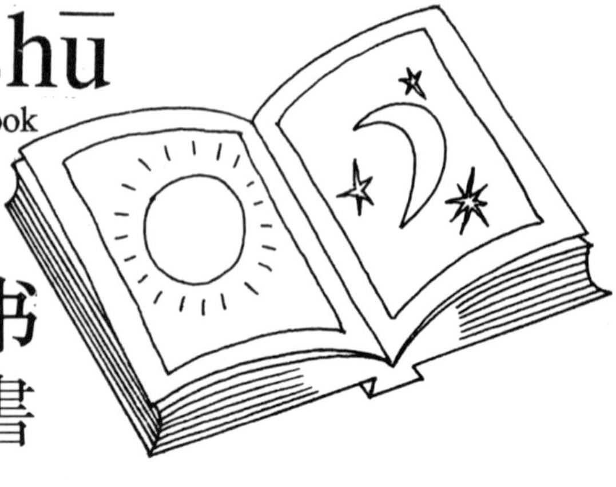

书
書

旧纸篓
舊紙簍

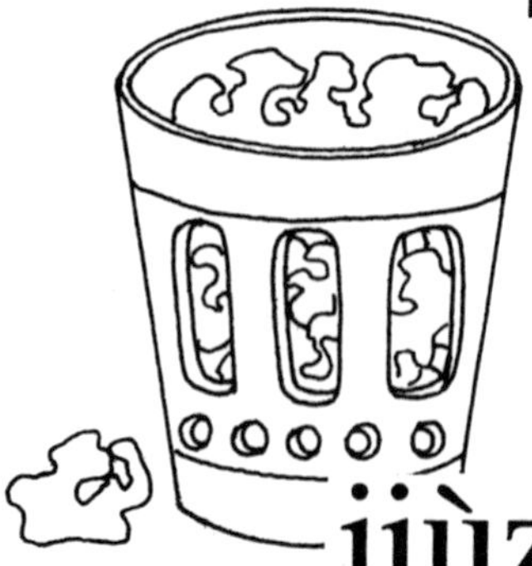

wastepaper basket jiùzhǐlǒu

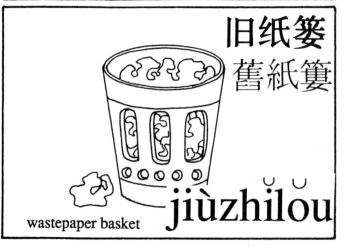

Nature

zǎochén	zāng	niǎo
zhōngwǔ	gānjìng	xiǎoshān
wǎnshàng	yèzi	huǒ
tàiyáng	huā	gǒu
xīngxing	shù	māo
yuèliang	shān	jīnyú
yǔ	pùbù	xióngmāo
fēng	shítou	shuǐ niú
jiēdào	hé	zìxíngchē

早晨 **zǎochén**

morning

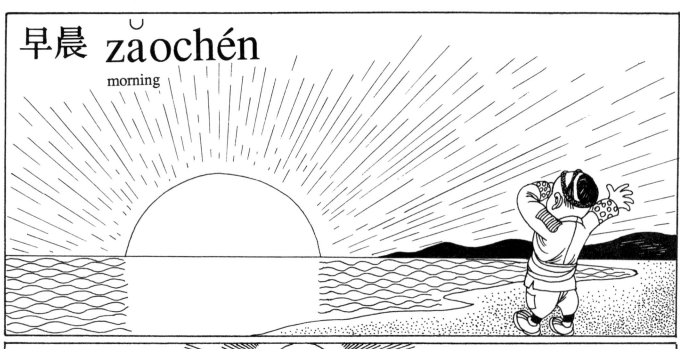

中午

zhōngwǔ

noon

晚上 **wǎnshàng**

evening

太阳 tàiyáng
太陽 sun

星星 xīngxing
star

月亮 yuèliang
moon

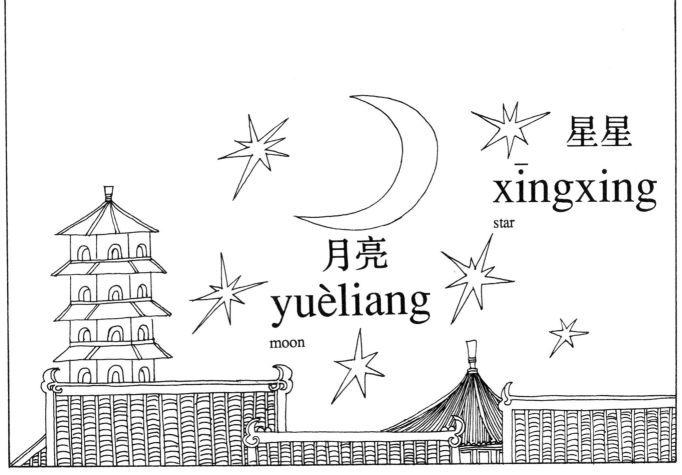

雨 yǔ
rain

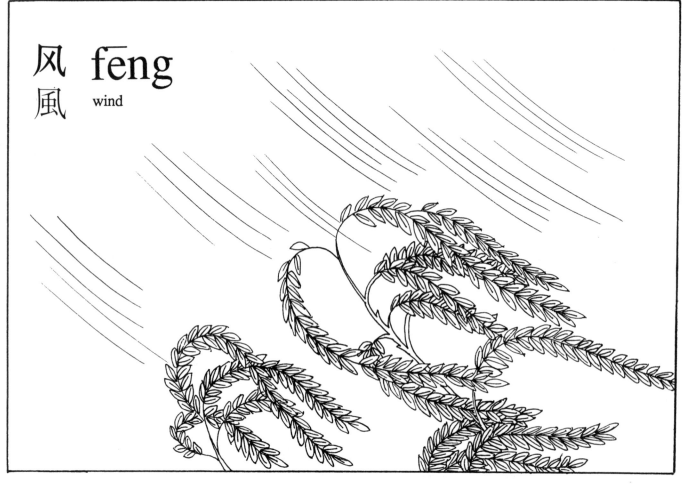

风
風 fēng
wind

街道 jiēdào

street

脏
髒 zāng   dirty

干净
乾淨
gānjìng

clean

山 shān
mountain

shítou 石头
stone 石頭

河 hé
river

瀑布
pùbù
waterfall

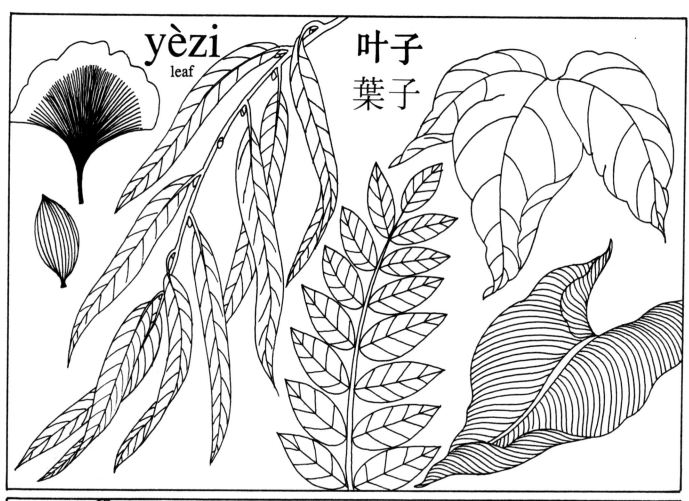

yèzi
leaf

叶子
葉子

花 huā
flower

树 **shù**
樹 tree

niǎo
bird

鸟

鳥

小山
xiǎoshān

火 huǒ
fire

火 huǒ
fire

狗 gǒu
dog

猫 māo
貓 cat

金鱼
金魚

jīnyú
goldfish

水牛
shuǐ niú
water buffalo

xióngmāo

熊猫
熊貓

panda

自行車
zìxíngchē bicycle

Chinese Glossary

ǎi — short

bā — eight
bái — white
bèi — back
bízi — nose
bōlí bēi — glass
bù gāoxìng — sad

cānjīn — napkin
chá — tea
Chángchéng —Great Wall
chángtǒng wà — stockings
chángzi — intestines
chǎngfáng — factory
chāzi — fork
chènyī — shirt
chéngshì — city
chǒu — ugly
chuānghù — window
chuáng — bed

dà — big
dàye — uncle
diànhuà — telephone
diànshìjī — television
dìtú — map
dǒng — understand

èr — two
ěrduō — ear
èrshí — twenty
érzi — son

fángzi — building
fěnbǐ — chalk
fēng — wind
fùqīn — father

gān — liver
gāngbǐ — pen
gānjìng — clean
gāo — tall
gāoxìng — happy
gēbo — arm
gěi — give
gōnggòng qìchē — bus
gōngrén — worker
gōngzuò — work
gǒu — dog

hē — drink
hé — river
hēibǎn — blackboard
hēibǎncā— eraser

hóng — red
hòu — last
hòubiān — behind
huā — flower
huáng — yellow
huǒ — fire

jī — chicken
jiā — house
jiān — shoulder
jiǎo — foot
jiǎozhǐ— toe
jīdàn — eggs
jiēdào — street
jǐgǔ — backbone
jīnyú — goldfish
jìn — near
jiǔ — nine
jiù — old
jiùzhǐlǒu — wastepaper basket
jú — orange

júzi — orange
kàn — see
kuàizi — chopsticks
kùzi — trousers

lái — come
lán — blue
lǎoshī — teacher
lěng — cold
lǐbiān — in
líng — zero
liù — six
lǜ — green

māo — cat
màozi — hat
měi — beautiful
mén — door
mén — gate
miào — temple
miànbāo — bread
mǐfàn — rice
mǔqīn — mother

nǎinai — grandmother
nánháizi — boy
nánrén — man
niǎo — bird
nóngchǎng — farm
nóngmín — farmer
nǚér — daughter
nǚháizi — girl
nǚrén — woman

pàng — fat
pánzi — plate
pǎo — run
pǐncháng — taste

píngguǒ — apple
pùbù — waterfall
qī — seven
qiánbāo — purse
qiānbǐ — pencil
qiánbiān — in front
qīng — light
qù — go

rè — hot
rénmén — people

sān — three
shān — mountain
shàngbiān — above
sháozi — spoon
shēntǐ — body
shí — ten
shíèr — twelve
shítou — stone
shíyī — eleven
shǒu — hand
shòu — thin
shǒujuàn — handkerchief
shǒuzhǐ — finger
shōuyīnjī — radio
shǔ — count
shū — book
shù — tree
shūzhuō — desk
shuǐ — water
shuǐ niú — water buffalo
shuō — speak
sì — four

tǎ — pagoda
tàiyáng — sun
tāng — soup
tǎngxià — lie down
tǎnzi — rug
tiào — jump
tīng — hear
tīng — listen
tóu — head
tóufa — hair
túhuà — picture
tuǐ — leg

wàibiān — out
wǎnshàng — evening
wǔ — five

xī — knee
xiàba — chin
xiàbiān — below
xié — shoes
xiān — first
xiāngjiāo — banana
xiǎo — small
xiǎoqìchē — car
xiǎoshān — hill
xīn — new
xīngxing — star
xīnzàng — heart
xiōngkǒu — chest
xióngmāo — panda

yā — duck
yǎnjīng — eye

yǎnjìng — glasses
yéye — grandfather
yèzi — leaf
yìbǎi — one hundred
yímā — aunt
yī — one
yīngér — baby
yìqiān — one thousand
yíwàn — ten thousand
yǐzi — chair
yóuyǒng — swim
yú — fish
yǔ — rain
yuǎn — far
yuèliang — moon

zǎochén — morning
zāng — dirty
zhǐ — paper
zhàn — stand
zhěntóu — pillow
zhōng — clock
zhòng — heavy
zhōng jiān — between
zhōngwǔ — noon
zǒu — walk
zhū — pig
zhūbǎo — jewelry
zhuōzi — table
zǐ — purple
zìxíngchē — bicycle
zuǐ — mouth
zuò — sit

English Glossary

above — shàngbiān
apple — píngguǒ
arm — gēbo
aunt — yímā

baby — yīngér
back — bèi
backbone — jǐgǔ
banana — xiāngjiāo
beautiful — měi
bed — chuáng
behind — hòubiān
below — xiàbiān
between — zhōngbiān
bicycle — zìxíngchē
big — dà
bird — niǎo
blackboard — hēibǎn
blue — lán
body — shēntǐ
book — shū
boy — nánháizi
bread — miànbāo
building — fángzi
bus — gōnggòng qìchē

car — xiǎoqìchē
cat — māo
chair — yǐzi
chalk — fěnbǐ
chest — xiōngkǒu
chicken — jī
chin — xiàba
chopsticks — kuàizi
city — chéngshì
clean — gānjìng
clock — zhōng
cold — lěng

come — lái
count — shǔ

daughter — nǚér
desk — shūzhuō
dirty — zāng
dog — gǒu
door — mén
drink — hē
duck — yā

ear — ěrduō
eggs — jīdàn
eight — bā
eleven — shíyī
eraser — hēibǎncā
evening — wǎnshàng
eye — yǎnjǐng

factory — chǎngfáng
far — yuǎn
farm — nóngchǎng
farmer — nóngmín
fat — pàng
father — fùqīn
finger — shǒuzhǐ
fire — huǒ
first — xiān
fish — yú
five — wǔ
flower — huā
foot — jiǎo
fork — chāzi
four — sì

gate — mén
girl — nǚháizi
give — gěi

glass — bōlí bēi
glasses — yǎnjìng
go — qù
goldfish — jīnyú
grandfather — yéye
grandmother — nǎinai
Great Wall, The —Chángchéng
green — lǜ

hair — tóufa
hand — shǒu
handkerchief — shǒujuàn
happy — gāoxìng
hat — màozi
head — tóu
hear — tīng
heart — xīnzàng
heavy — zhòng
hill — xiǎoshān
hot — rè
house — jiā

in — lǐbiān
in front — qiánbiān
intestines — chángzi

jewelry — zhūbǎo
jump — tiào

knee — xī

last — hòu
leaf — yèzi
leg — tuǐ
lie down — tǎngxià
light — qīng
listen — tīng
liver — gān

94

man — nánrén

map — dìtú

moon — yuèliang

morning — zǎochén

mother — mǔqīn

mountain — shān

mouth — zuǐ

napkin — cānjīn

near — jìn

new — xīn

nine — jiǔ

noon — zhōngwǔ

nose — bízi

old — jìu

one — yī

one hundred — yìbǎi

one thousand — yìqiān

orange — júzi

orange — jú

out — wàibiān

pagoda — tǎ

panda — xióngmāo

paper — zhǐ

pen — gāngbǐ

pencil — qiānbǐ

people — rénmén

picture — túhuà

pig — zhū

pillow — zhěntóu

plate — pánzi

purple — zǐ

purse — qiánbāo

radio — shōuyīnjī

rain — yǔ

red — hóng

rice — mǐfàn

river — hé

rug — tǎnzi

run — pǎo

sad — bù gāoxìng

see — kàn

seven — qī

shirt — chènyī

shoes — xié

short — ǎi

shoulder — jiān

sit — zuò

six — liù

small — xiǎo

son — érzi

soup — tāng

speak — shuō

spoon — sháozi

stand — zhàn

star — xīngxing

stockings — chángtǒng wà

stomach — wèi

stone — shítou

street — jiēdào

sun — tàiyáng

swim — yóuyǒng

table — zhuōzi

tall — gāo

taste — pǐncháng

tea — chá

teacher — lǎoshī

telephone — diànhuà

television — diànshìjī

temple — miào

ten — shí

ten thousand — yíwàn

thin — shòu

three — sān

toe — jiǎozhǐ

tree — shù

trousers — kùzi

twelve — shíèr

twenty — èrshí

two — èr

ugly — chǒu

uncle — dàye

understand — dǒng

walk — zǒu

wastepaper basket — jiùzhǐlǒu

water — shuǐ

water buffalo — shuǐ niú

waterfall — pùbù

white — bái

wind — fēng

window — chuānghù

woman — nǚrén

work — gōngzuò

worker — gōngrén

yellow — huáng

zero — líng